Dedication

To Rachel.

BEGINNER'S GUIDE TO Needle Felting

BEGINNER'S GUIDE TO
Needle Felting

Susanna Wallis

SEARCH PRESS

First published in Great Britain 2008

Search Press Limited
Wellwood, North Farm Road,
Tunbridge Wells, Kent TN2 3DR

Reprinted 2009, 2010, 2012 (twice)

Text and needlework designs copyright © Susanna Wallis 2008

Photographs by Debbie Patterson at Search Press Studios
Photographs and design copyright © Search Press Ltd 2008

ISBN: 978-1-84448-251-1

The Publishers and author can accept no responsibility for any
consequences arising from the information, advice or instructions
given in this publication.

Readers are permitted to reproduce any of the designs in this
book for their personal use, or for the purposes of selling for
charity, free of charge and without the prior permission of the
Publishers. Any use of the designs for commercial purposes is not
permitted without the prior permission of the Publishers.

Suppliers

If you have difficulty in obtaining any of the materials and
equipment mentioned in this book, then please visit the Search
Press website for details of suppliers: www.searchpress.com

Publisher's note
All the step-by-step photographs in this book feature the
author, Susanna Wallis, demonstrating needle felting. No
models have been used.

Printed in Malaysia

Acknowledgements

I would like to thank James, my partner and my
daughter Rachel; my parents, family and friends,
especially Tina and Karin; and fellow feltmaker
Mechtild, for all being so generous and full of
encouragement. Thanks to tutors Viv at the
Adult College and Michelle at Greenwich Craft
Foundation, who started me on the route to felting
success. Thanks to Search Press for giving me
this great opportunity and to The Handweavers
Studio, wizpick.com and knitshop.co.uk for essential
information and supplies.

Page 1
*There are full instructions for making this Dotty Bird on pages
40–45.*

Page 3
This is a variation on the Heart Card shown on pages 22–25.

Opposite
*You can learn how to make a cup and saucer on pages 48–53.
The project is shown here with some colourful alternatives.*

Contents

Introduction

Needle felting is an exciting and versatile hobby; all around the world crafters are discovering how amazing it is to sculpt wool with a specialised needle. Now it is your turn! The projects in this book will introduce you to several easy steps, enabling you to produce a variety of designs, and will inspire you to experiment further with your own ideas. No specialist sculpting skills are required, just a willingness to explore a new craft.

Needle felting has evolved from feltmaking, which was a vital skill in many ancient cultures throughout the world, where there was the need for warm clothing, blankets, shoes and even tents made out of wool. Feltmaking is found in all countries where sheep are herded and is the oldest form of fabric production, pre-dating spinning, weaving and knitting. To make felt fabric, sheep's wool is washed, combed and laid out, usually on a large, flat surface. Moisture and friction are then applied. Natural animal fibres such as wool have microscopic scales which lie in one direction; the purpose of this is to keep moisture and debris away from the skin of the animal. The action of warmth, moisture and friction on these fibres causes them to bond. Once fully bonded (fulled), the fabric can be cut and sewn into various items and will not fray. Historic examples of feltmaking can be found in museums worldwide.

In needle felting, the fulling process is done solely by the action of a barbed needle being moved to bond the fibres into a firm surface or structure. In the Industrial Revolution (mid to late 1800s) in Western Europe, large feltmaking machines were developed to speed up the production of felt to make carpets, mattresses, and insulation. The machines are still used, with thousands of needles using friction alone to bond fibres into fabric. There is also now a table-top version for home use, sometimes called an embellishing machine, and the needles in these machines are the same as you will find available for needle felting.

Needle felting as a craft and method of sculpting is very young, with some suggestions of origins in the USA in the 1980s. It is becoming very popular in Europe and the USA and there are many devotees to be found at craft events, in internet forums and in groups such as the International Feltmakers Association.

After first learning flat felting, I thought that I would never be able to go on to sculpt wool nor get used to felting with a needle. It did not take long, however, to become absorbed in the excitement of a project developing before my own eyes and how magical it is to make something so unique out of a very basic raw material. I sincerely hope you become as captivated as I am by this addictive craft.

Materials

To begin needle felting, you will need just a few essential, inexpensive items. The basics are felting needles, a firm foam block, washed and sorted sheep's wool and carded, dyed wool, known as rovings or combed tops. There are now many suppliers that stock these essentials. Combed tops are becoming more available in general craft shops but are most often obtained from specialist weaving suppliers. The internet is an easy source of information on suppliers, for ordering of materials as well as forums on needle felting.

Wool

Raw wool

This wool is used primarily in this book for the internal structure of sculpted pieces. It felts quite quickly and firmly. It is the wool straight from the fleece of a sheep that has been shorn and the length of the wool fibres and how coarse or curly they are depends on the breed of sheep. If you are able to get wool direct from a farm you will need to sort, wash and comb the fleece before use. Some suppliers sell wool in this 'raw' condition or otherwise it can be bought ready sorted and washed, ready to use.

Sorting the wool involves grading it into different usable or non-usable sections and removing mud and debris from the fleece. If washing the wool, place it in a large container of water. Do not stir it or add detergent, but just keep changing the water until it becomes clear. Allow the wool to dry naturally. Once dry, comb the wool using the carders as described on pages 20–21, or use a drum carder if you have one. Carding the wool combs the fibres into long strips (known as slivers), ready to be felted. Continue to remove any remaining debris and set aside the combed wool ready to use for projects.

Rovings

Rovings/combed wool is graded, sorted, washed, carded, and finally dyed. The most popular wool used for feltmaking tends to be merino, as it felts easily, is very soft and has a subtle sheen. It originates from Australia and New Zealand and is widely available from suppliers. The disadvantage of using finer wools is that needle holes may show up on the finished item.

Needles

Felting needles are made from carbon steel and come in various sizes (gauges) and lengths. Depending on the supplier, the gauges can be described in number format or simply as fine, medium, and large. A 32 gauge is a thicker needle, best used on coarse wool, but it can require a lot of hard jabbing. The 36 and 38 gauges are the most commonly used, all-purpose needles, and the 42 gauge is a very fine needle which is ideal for delicate, detailed work but quite fragile to work with.

The choice of gauge is quite individual to each feltmaker; it is best to experiment with different gauges to see which you prefer. Some feltmakers like to begin with larger needles when using coarse (raw) wool and then move on to finer needles when using finer wool, as this reduces the look of needle holes on the finished item.

The needles are very sharp and as this book is not an acupuncture manual, it is advisable to avoid distractions and not to watch television whilst needle felting! The needles are strong and can last for a long time but they are breakable and it is a matter of getting used to the feel of the needles and of how light or heavy you can be with your felting movements.

A close-up photograph of a felting needle shows the grooves on the shaft of each needle. These grooves, or barbs, enable the needle to 'grab' the individual wool fibres and pull them through to bond to the adjoining fibres and subsequently sculpt the fibres into a firm, finished piece. The range of felting needles available also includes needles with variations in the position and number of barbs on the needle shaft, giving very specific and detailed results.

Needle holders

There are various needle holders on the market and they can be found at all needle felting suppliers. It can be down to individual choice whether you wish to use a holder for your projects. Some feltmakers find them more comfortable to use than holding the needle itself. Holders can be for a single needle or multiple needles and should hold different gauge needles depending on individual requirements.

Tip

Some suppliers colour code the top of their different sized needles for easy recognition. You can do this yourself with enamel paints or nail varnish.

A close-up photograph of a felting needle, showing the barbs.

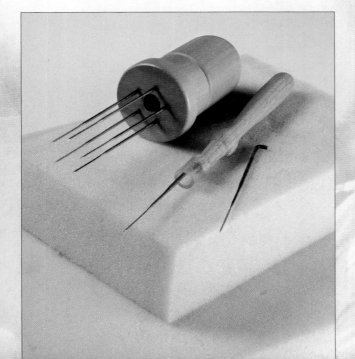

Foam block

In order to use the needle correctly, you need to be able to jab it down into the wool, and to avoid injury to yourself and possible damage to furniture, it is essential to have a foam block: a firm sponge about 20 x 20cm (8 x 8in) placed under your work as protection. Again these may be bought from specialist suppliers, or you could use any firm foam block from a general craft or fabric shop. Larger projects will need larger foam sizes. Some suppliers stock a new variety of needle felting block that has bristles like an upturned brush and there are specific needles that accompany this product, so do check with your chosen supplier when purchasing. One advantage of this version is that it will not shed bits of foam, which can happen with other foam blocks when they get well used.

Other materials

Carders These are combs that are commonly used in wool sorting and preparation for spinning and feltmaking. They are used to remove debris from the wool and to comb the fibres into the same direction ready to be spun or felted. Carders come in a set of two and are held one in each hand. (There is no right or left preference – use whichever hand suits you.) They are available in different sizes; strangely the smaller sized carders are actually the same product as dog/cat combs so are available to buy from your local pet shop! Larger wooden carders can be purchased from weaving suppliers. There are angled wire bristles on each carder and in each set of two carders the bristles line up in opposite directions.

Artboards and canvas frames These are pre-prepared backings for art projects and collages. Artboards are flat, sturdy boards covered with canvas. Canvas frames are made with treated canvas stretched over a wooden frame. There are many sizes to suit your particular project and both are available from all good art stores. Finished work can be glued on to the canvas background using craft or wood glue.

Card blanks These can be bought in a kit or can be made from good quality card. There are many stores and online suppliers that offer various colours and textures of card and there are many types of card shape and aperture to suit particular projects.

Clear elastic This is a strong, stretchy thread for use in jewellery projects. It is sold on a roll and is available in a variety of colours and thicknesses. It can be purchased from good bead shops and craft suppliers. A long darning-type needle is ideal to use with this thread.

Threads and beads Cotton thread and embroidery silks are commonly found in sewing shops, as are seed and bugle beads. Regular sewing needles are used with the threads in this book, though you may need to use a beading (fine) needle to attach the smaller beads.

Thimble This will protect your finger from getting sore when doing a lot of sewing. Buy it from sewing stores.

Round-nosed jewellery pliers These are generally used in jewellery projects and are a valuable tool for any craft kit. They are available from good beads shops and craft suppliers.

Bird's legs The ones used in the Dotty Bird project were bought ready-made from a European craft supplier but an alternative would be to make legs using a fine gauge but strong craft wire and jewellery pliers.

Scissors Medium-sized, sharp fabric scissors are ideal for all the projects shown and can be bought from sewing shops or hardware stores.

PVA glue Strong craft PVA glue or wood glue is ideal for all the projects in the book.

Pipe cleaners These are used for making armatures as shown on pages 18–19. I find that the original pipe cleaners (not the children's craft versions) are best, as they are less 'furry' and thinner. These are available from tobacconists.

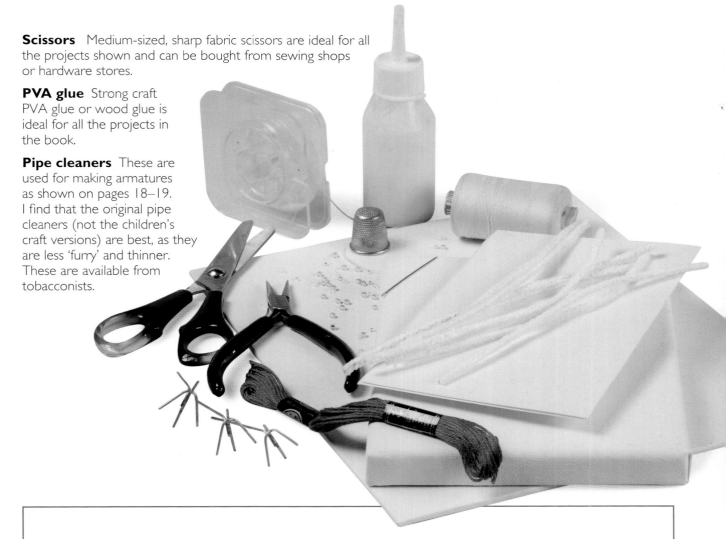

Safety, posture and care while felting

Needle felting can be a very absorbing, some would say even slightly addictive hobby, so before starting there are a few points to consider. Because the needles are so sharp, it is highly important that needles are stored appropriately after use and disposed of carefully if they break.

Keep needles away from children, animals and unsuspecting partners! Suppliers may dispatch needles in a sturdy plastic box; alternatively you could use a small, strong cardboard box or felt-lined tin to keep needles in. Always replace needles in storage immediately if pausing to answer the phone etc. and after use.

It is important to develop good postural habits and find a comfortable position to work in, whether at a table or in an armchair.

Always have a foam block under the item you are working on. If you are sitting in an armchair, you could place an old cushion beneath the foam block to raise your work to a comfortable working height.

Unless you intend to needle felt for several hours a day, you should not develop a repetitive strain injury.

Basic techniques

Needling

This is the fun but occasionally painful part! Hold your project in one hand, resting your wrist on the foam block and with the other hand holding the needle comfortably. Begin to jab at the wool, following the instructions in each project. Always pay great attention to avoiding jabbing yourself with the needle. Keep the needle as far as possible from your fingers. If you do jab yourself, put an ice cube on the affected area for a few minutes.

The needling action itself is a small wrist/forearm movement. This will produce quite quick results on a small area of wool, forcing the wool to knit tightly together.

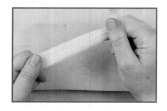

1 Pull off a wisp of merino wool and pull it between your hands to thin it.

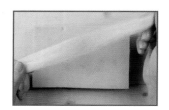

2 Pull the wisp of wool apart in this way.

3 Lay a thinned piece of wool on your foam block as shown.

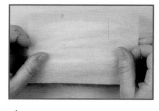

4 Continue adding wool until you have a thin layer across the foam block.

5 Keep on layering the wool until you have a layer around 1cm (³/₈in) thick.

6 Take the multiple needle holder and stab through the wool and into the foam block. The barbed felting needles pull the fibres through each other and they bond together.

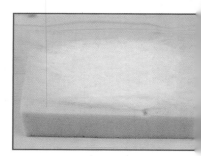

7 Continue stabbing repeatedly through the wool all over the layer until it is bonded together.

 **8** Fold over the wispy edges of the wool to make a more definite shape.

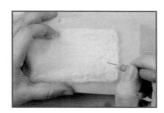 **9** Take a single needle and define the edges further by needling.

 **10** The shape of the background should now be flatter and more compact.

 **11** Turn the picture round, take a piece of merino wool in the petal colour and pull it into thin wisps.

 **12** Place the wisp on the picture in a petal shape.

 **13** Needle the petal, pulling it into shape as you go.

 **14** Add more petals in the same way. Take a thin wisp of merino wool in the centre colour.

 **15** Place the wisp in the centre and needle it in place.

 **16** Pull a thin wisp of green merino wool and lay it on the picture as the flower stalk.

 **17** Lay down and needle another green wisp to create a leaf. Make a second leaf in the same way.

 **18** Gently pull the picture off the foam block.

The finished picture.

Making a ball shape

The making of a ball shape enables the feltmaker to extend potential ideas for future projects as there are so many possibilities to develop from this technique. The felted balls can be as small or large as you wish and can be decorated in a number of ways, plain or patterned. You will be able to make jewellery, decorations, toys and lots more.

1 Take a handful of raw, uncombed wool, as this is coarse and bonds together more quickly.

2 Use the needle to begin pushing the fibres into a loose ball shape.

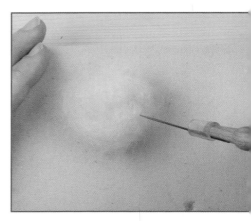

3 Turn the ball as you shape it in this way.

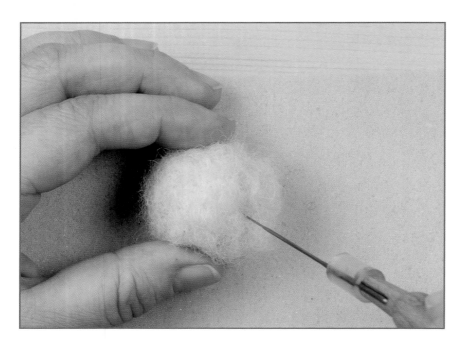

4 Hold the ball in place and carefully needle it to condense it into a tighter shape.

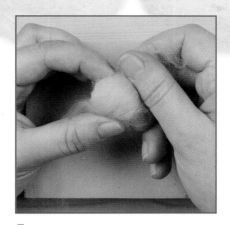

5 Take a wisp of merino wool in the top colour and wrap it round the ball shape.

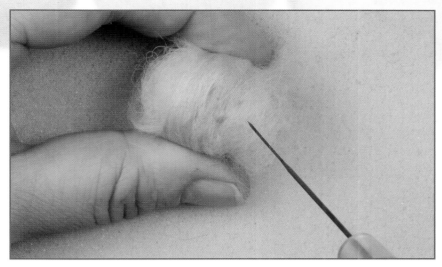

6 Secure the top colour with a few stabs of the needle.

7 Add more wisps and continue, needling and turning the ball as you go.

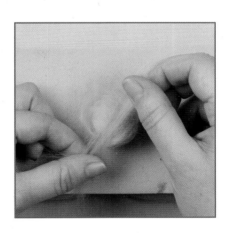

8 Continue until the ball is well covered.

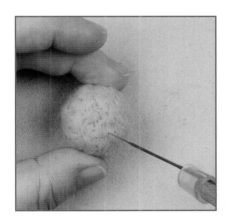

A selection of finished felt balls.

Shape forming

Exciting designs can be developed by forming wool into vessels, dishes etc., allowing you to extend your skills in sculpting wool. Definition and shaping can be achieved by needling for longer on particular areas of the piece. Designs could be used as fun ornaments, containers and miniature gift or treasure boxes. Why not get inspiration from historic or contemporary decorative styles to beautify your design! This demonstration shows how to make a saucer.

1 Take a thick length of merino wool and lay it in a coil shape.

2 When you have a circle of the size you want, tear off the excess.

3 Begin needling the coil to neaten the shape.

4 Continue needling to form the shape.

5 Lay a wisp of the same wool over the top to cover the needle marks.

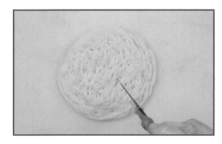

6 Continue adding more wisps to cover the coil shape, and needle to bond and strengthen the edges.

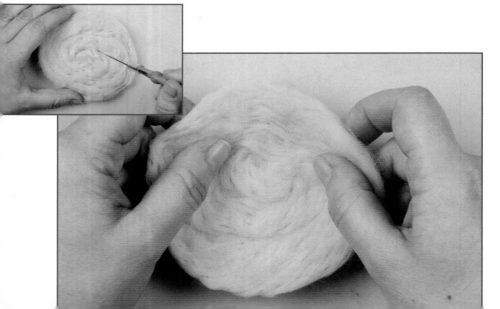

7 Turn the piece over and needle the other side as before. Then begin to form the circle into a saucer shape.

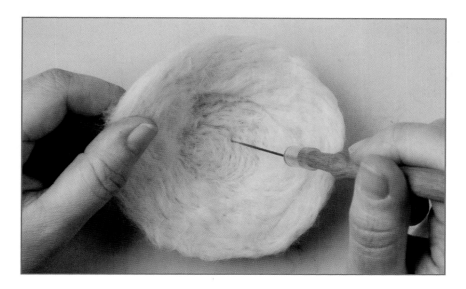

8 Needle in the middle of the shape to form it, beginning to define a dip in the centre.

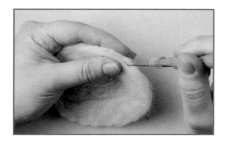

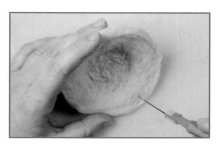

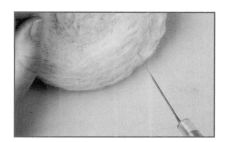

9 Once a defined shape has been achieved, hold the edge between your fingers and very carefully needle to create a firm rim.

10 Tilt the saucer and needle the rim to firm up the edges.

11 Create fluff to hide the needling holes by brushing the needle over the fibres.

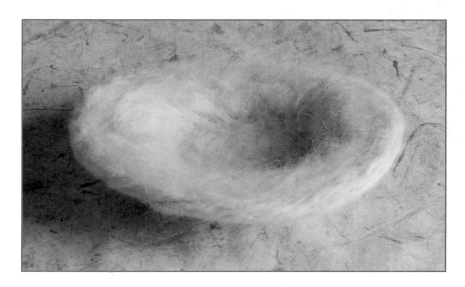

The finished saucer, ready for further decoration.

Using an armature

An armature is like a skeletal structure within a sculpted design. Using pipe cleaners or wire to build an armature allows for diverse shapes to be formed and therefore many more design opportunities. Structures with an armature can be stronger and more stable and can have limbs, etc. An armature will also allow for the item to be gently repositioned.

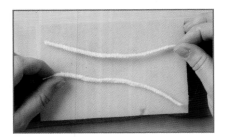

1 Take two old-fashioned, cotton-covered pipe cleaners and lay them on your foam block.

2 Twist the pipe cleaners together in a cross shape as shown.

3 Twists the ends together and form each side into a butterfly's wing.

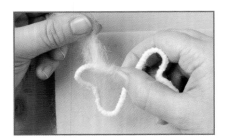

4 Take wisps of raw wool and begin to wrap them round the butterfly armature.

5 Go all round the armature, wrapping it with the wool.

6 Place the shape on the foam block and begin to needle it, being careful not to stab the pipe cleaner armature with the needle.

7 Lift the piece off the foam block, turn it over and work on the other side, adding more wool as necessary.

8 Take a wisp of coloured merino wool and wrap it round the butterfly shape.

9 Needle the wisp into the butterfly and continue adding wool and needling to cover the piece.

10 Continue needling to form the shape.

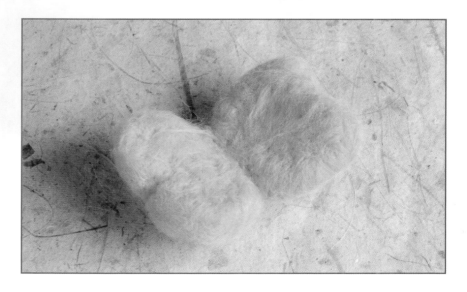

The finished butterfly shape, ready for decoration.

Carding wool to blend colours

There is a rainbow of colours of rovings available from suppliers. Some feltmakers dye their own wool and beautiful colours can be achieved by producing your own plant dyes. You may wish to extend the range of colours you have by blending different rovings together using the carders. I like to do this as sumptuous and rich variations in tone can be achieved by mixing two or three colours together.

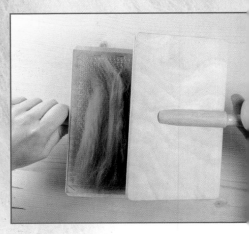

1 Place the left-hand carder facing upwards and the right-hand one facing downwards. Reverse this if you are left-handed. Pull thin wisps of three very slightly different shades of merino wool and lay them on to the left-hand carder.

2 Hold the carders by the handles and hold the right-hand one over the left-hand one.

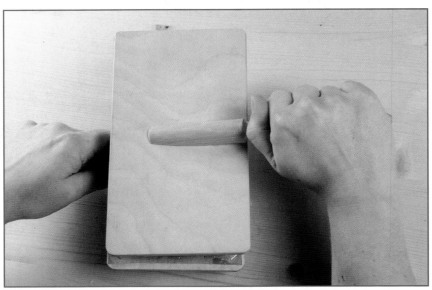

3 Push the carders together as shown.

20

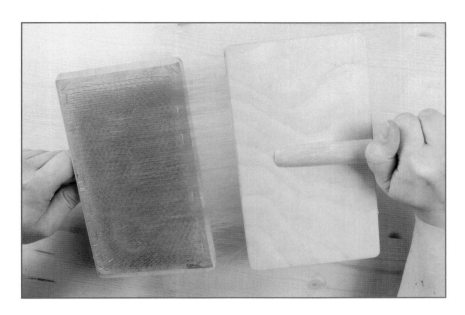

4 Pull the carders apart so that the wool is pulled through the teeth. Repeat and continue.

5 Remove the wool by holding the carders upright and combing one down the other as shown. Repeat until the wool comes free.

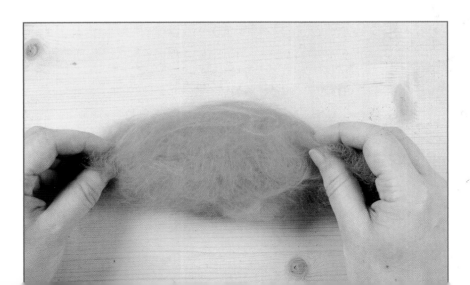

The blended wool.

Heart Card

It is always a delight to receive a handmade card and this needle-felted design is a simple but stunning project to kick-start your card making skills.

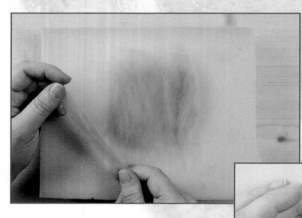

1 Lay wisps of the blended turquoise wool on the foam block to create the background.

You will need

- Merino wool in shades of bright turquoise, blended
- Light turquoise merino wool
- Foam block
- Felting needle
- Silver seed beads
- Beading needle and thread
- Card blank
- PVA glue

2 Needle the background, add more wool and continue needling to shape into a rectangle.

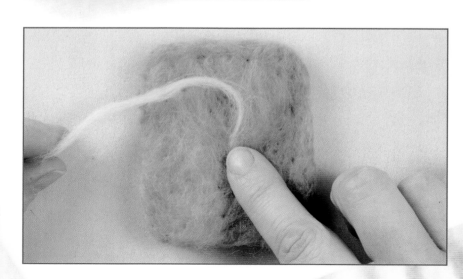

3 Take a thin wisp of light turquoise merino wool and shape it into half of a heart shape on the background.

4 Needle the first half of the heart shape to embed it in the background.

5 Add the second half of the heart in the same way, then place more wisps of wool over the middle of the heart and needle them to fill the heart in.

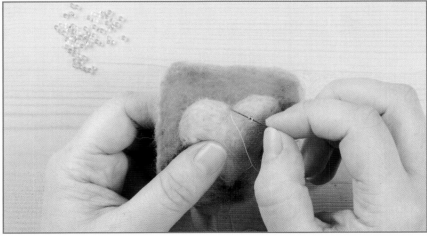

6 Thread a beading needle with ordinary sewing thread and knot the end. Come up through the back of the piece at the edge of the heart and pick up a seed bead. Go down again through the edge of the heart.

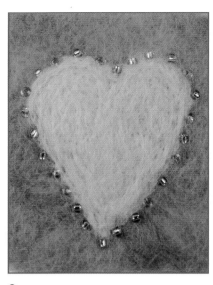

7 Take the needle down through the piece, come up further along the heart's edge, pick up another seed bead and continue all round the edge.

8 Sew beads on all round the edge of the heart.

9 Place blobs of PVA glue around the edge of the back of the piece, and stick it to the card blank.

Opposite
The finished Heart Card.

Once you have mastered the Heart Card design, you will be able to experiment with more elaborate work, add pattern lines and vary sizes.

Country Picture

A miniature work of art can be made by using the wool like paint and producing a simple but very effective picture. Inspiration for your picture could come from a variety of sources: a favourite view or photograph, abstract or contemporary art, historic decorative designs or a botanical or other natural image.

You will need

- Merino wool in white, pale blue, dark green, olive green, golden green, yellow, bright green, brown and black
- Foam block
- Felting needle
- Scissors
- PVA glue
- Canvas frame, 13 × 18cm (5$\frac{1}{8}$ × 7$\frac{1}{8}$in)

1 Prepare a white merino wool base in an oval shape, 15cm (6in) high.

Tip
You could use needle-punched wool or wet felted merino to save time, instead of needle felting your own base for the picture.

2 Lay on wisps of the pale blue merino wool to begin the sky.

3 Needle the sky on, adding layers of wool as required. Fold in the fluffy edges. You will need around three layers of thin wisps for good coverage.

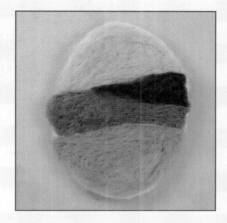

4 Next, add dark green merino for the background hill and needle it in place.

5 Next add the olive green wool for the field in the middle distance, and needle it in place as usual.

6 Add a layer of golden green for the foreground and needle it.

7 Begin to add details. Take thin wisps of yellow merino wool and lay them out to make the sun's rays. Needle them in. Do not worry if they go off the edge of the picture as they can be folded over or trimmed.

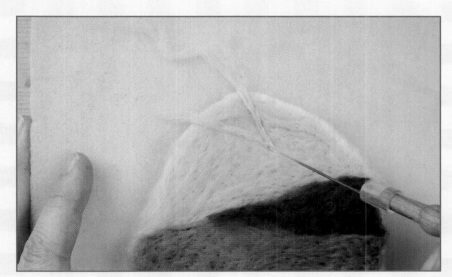

8 Add oval shapes in the background for the three distant trees in dark green and bright green merino wool.

9 Add blended green wools for the hedge. Take a thin wisp of brown wool and needle it in place to begin the gate.

10 Make a rectangle with two diagonals for the gate. Needle the thin lines of wool carefully.

11 Add more bushes in the hedge in different greens.

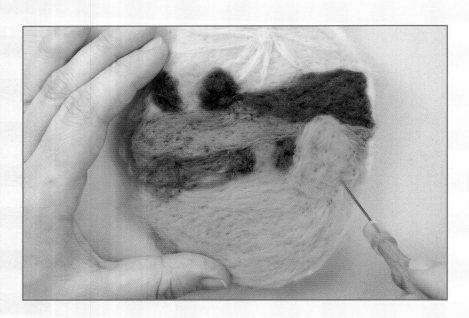

12 Needle on bright green wool for the foreground tree.

13 Place a wisp of brown merino wool for the tree trunk.

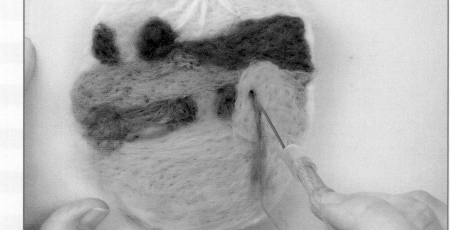

14 Add more wisps of brown wool and needle them in for branches.

15 To create a sheep, you need to start with a little cloud shape of white merino wool. Add a tiny wisp at a time.

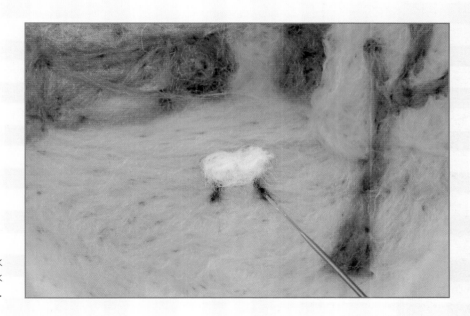

16 Add a tiny wisp of black merino wool for the sheep's back legs, and another for the front legs.

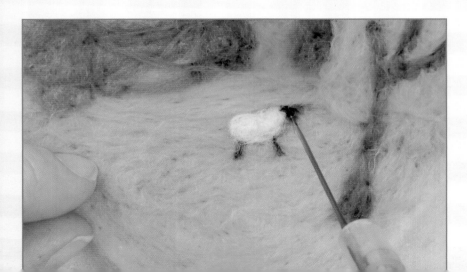

17 Add a triangle of black wool for the sheep's face.

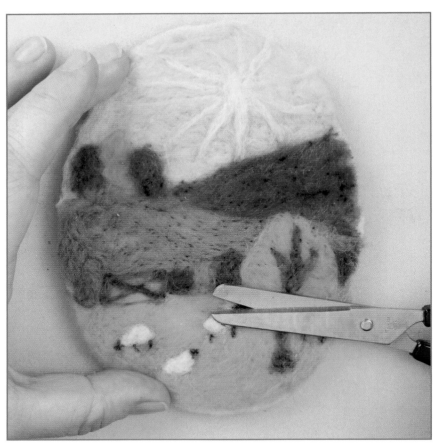

18 Add more sheep in the same way. If the picture looks too fluffy towards the end of the project, needle it all over.

19 Trim any stray fibres with scissors, particularly around details such as the black parts of the sheep.

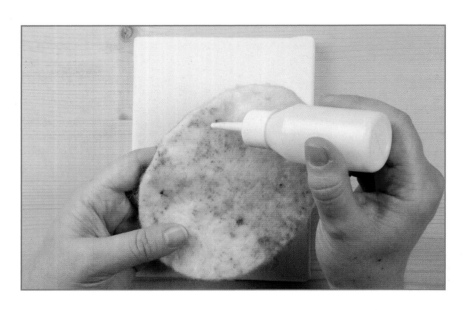

20 Use PVA glue to stick the picture on to the canvas frame.

Opposite
The finished Country Picture.

There are many design possibilities for pictures. Different effects can be achieved by using more than one layer of background colour. You could use a colour, a decorative shape or a design as initial points of inspiration. You can use thin strips of merino to create outlines and patterned effects, and add beads for an extra special finish.

Bracelet

These fun felted beads can be made into stunning bracelets, necklaces and earrings. You can be as adventurous as you wish with your design and make up colours and patterns to complement an outfit for a co-ordinated look.

You will need

- Raw, uncombed wool
- Merino wool in three or four colours
- Foam block
- Felting needle
- Clear elastic thread
- Darning needle
- Scissors
- PVA glue
- Thimble and jewellery pliers (optional)

1 Choose three or four colours of merino wool that will look good together.

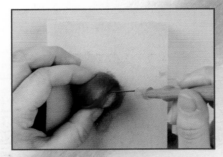

2 Make a ball using raw, uncombed wool as shown on page 14. Wrap a wisp of coloured merino wool around it and needle it in. Continue adding wisps and needling to cover the ball.

3 Work out how many balls you need to make a bracelet to go round the wearer's wrist. I have made nine.

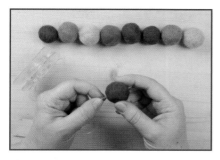  

4 Work out the order in which you want to thread the felt beads. Leaving the clear elastic thread on the reel, thread a darning needle and go through the first bead.

5 Continue threading. You can use a thimble if you need to. If the felt ball is very dense, you may need to pull the needle through using jewellery pliers.

6 Test the bracelet to see if it fits before adding the final beads. Then tie the clear elastic thread in a double knot.

Tip
To make the bracelet extra-strong, you can take the thread through all the felt beads for a second time before tying off.

7 Trim the ends of the clear elastic thread. Do not cut the ends too short at first.

8 Apply a little PVA glue to the knot to secure it. Let the glue dry and then retrim the ends of the thread if necessary.

Decorate beads with different patterns and add a key ring, a loop or a key fob to make these unique felted creations.

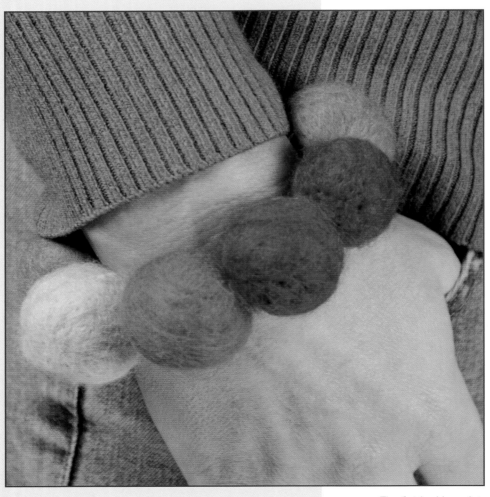

The finished bracelet.

You can vary the colours used to make a different bracelet, or decorate the beads with patterns for a striking effect.

Dotty Bird

This delightful bird is straightforward to make and further bird projects can be made in different sizes, in any colour and with a variety of patterns.

You will need

- Three pipe cleaners
- Scissors
- Foam block
- Raw wool
- Merino wool in deep blue and in many bright colours
- Wire legs and pen
- Large needle or safety pin

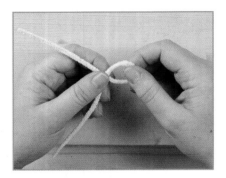

1 Twist the ends of two pipe cleaners together to make one long pipe cleaner. Twist it to make a loop for the bird's head.

2 Twist together the other ends of the pipe cleaner to make the bird's body shape.

3 Twist the end of a third pipe cleaner round one of the tail ends, and shape it to create the bird's tail. Twist it round the other tail end and trim off any excess pipe cleaner with scissors, making sure the sharp end is tucked away.

4 Wrap raw wool around the armature, as for the butterfly on pages 18–19.

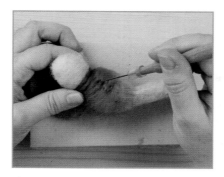

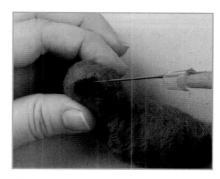

5 Continue wrapping the armature, stuffing it with raw wool and needling on the foam block to create the bird shape.

6 Begin to wrap the bird shape with the background colour and needle it in place.

7 Take a wisp of black and needle it in place to make one of the bird's eyes.

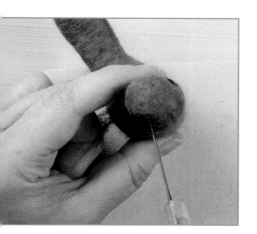

8 Create the second eye, making sure it is directly opposite the first one on the other side of the head.

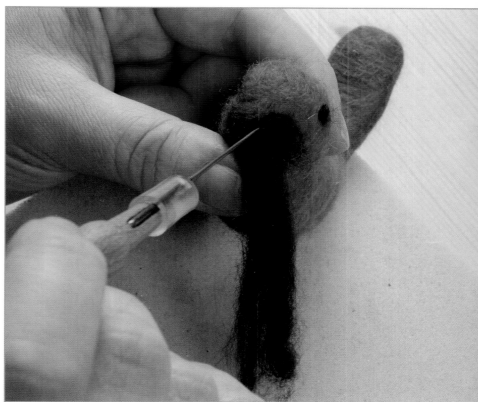

9 Take a larger wisp of black wool for the beak, and place it carefully in a good position, equidistant between the eyes.

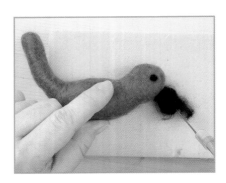

10 Secure the black wool with a few stabs of the needle to create the base of the beak, then begin to needle the beak itself.

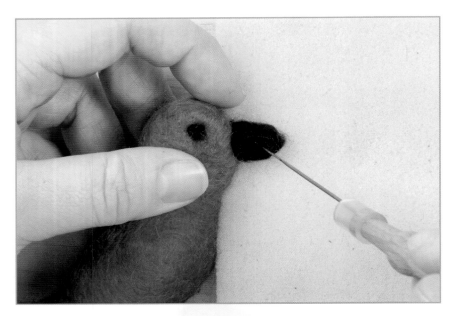

11 Needle to form a conical shape, turning the bird as you go to ensure that it is even.

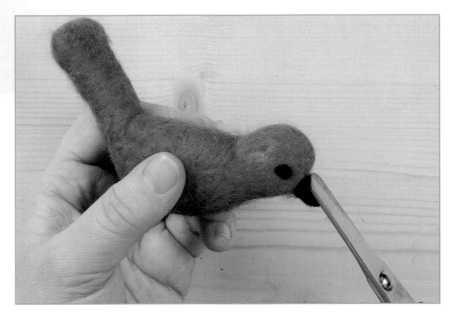

12 Gently trim the beak with scissors to shave off any stray fibres.

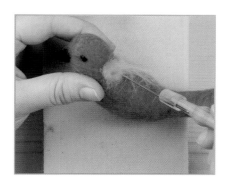

13 To create the bird's polka dots, choose thin wisps of brightly coloured merino wool. Begin to needle one in.

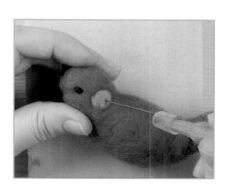

14 Continue needling to make a neat polka dot.

15 Cover the bird with polka dots in many different colours. Take the wire legs and hold them up against the bird to work out where they should go.

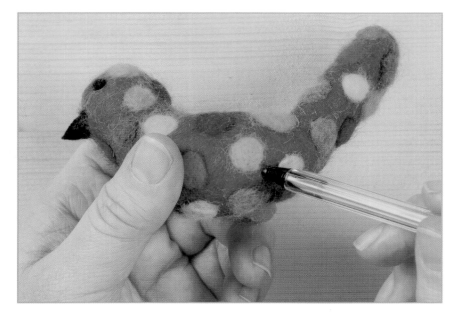

16 Mark with a pen where the legs should go.

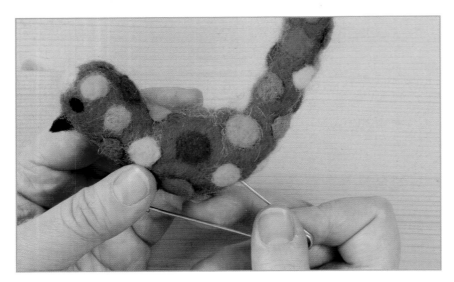

17 Make holes for the legs using a large needle or safety pin.

18 Apply a dot of PVA glue to each hole.

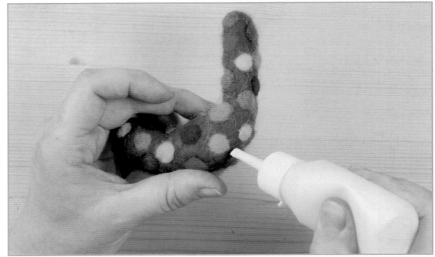

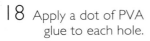

19 Push the legs into the holes to complete the bird.

Opposite
The finished Dotty Bird.

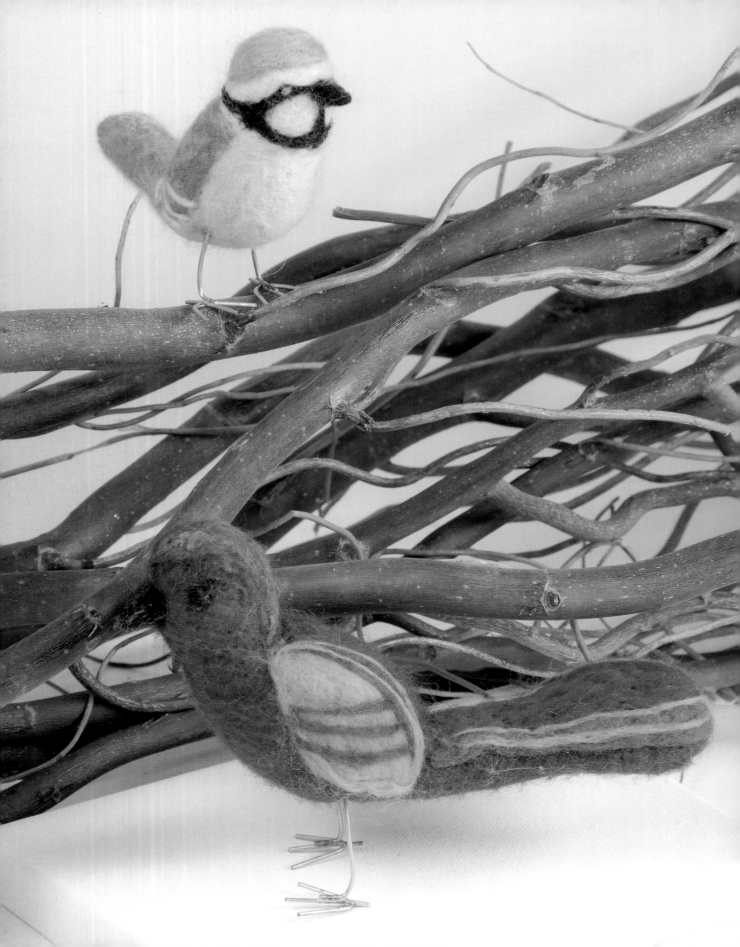

Birds can be made in a variety of styles, either from your imagination or as a life-like study of a recognised breed, and they can be free-standing or made without legs to be used as a mobile or hanging decoration.

Cup and Saucer

These whimsical cups and saucers are great fun and can be just for ornamental use or could be a special tea set for children who are beyond the age of eating or breaking their toys!

You will need

- Merino wool in blue, pale pink, purple and dark green
- Foam block
- Felting needle
- Foam cut into cup former
- Scissors

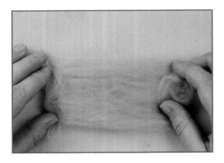

1 Make a thick layer of blue merino wool in a rectangle of around 4 × 10cm (1⅝ × 4in). It should be 1cm (³⁄₈in) thick.

2 Needle to firm up the shape.

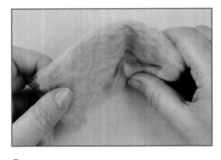

3 Take the rectangle off the foam block and curve it round from one end.

4 Continue curving the piece round to make a cup shape.

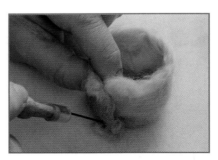

5 Needle round the base to hold the cup shape together.

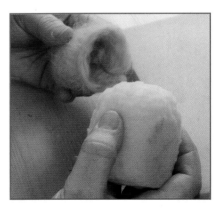

6 Take a piece of foam cut into a former for cup shapes.

7 Squeeze the former into the felted cup shape. Needle the felt to secure the seam.

8 Add more wool to cover the seam and any parts that feel thin. Needle the shape.

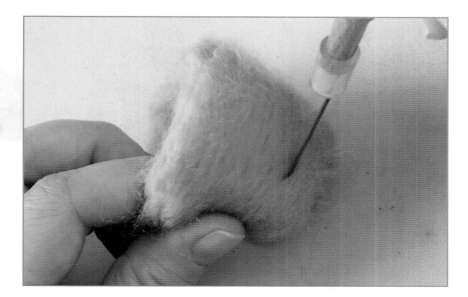

9 Remove the cup from the former. Hold it in your hand and needle it carefully to firm up the shape. Add wool as necessary.

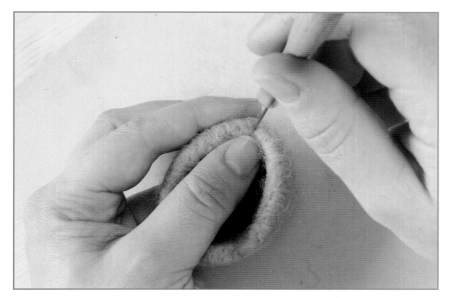

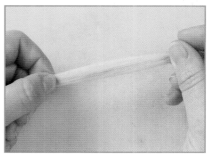

10 Hold the rim of the cup between your finger and thumb and needle it carefully to firm it up.

11 Take a wisp of the same blue wool for the handle.

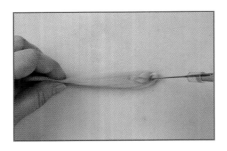

12 Fold over the ends of the wisp and needle.

13 Continue needling until the shape is firmer and add more layers of wool by wrapping them round the handle.

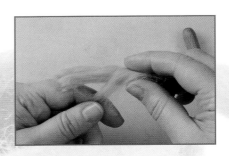

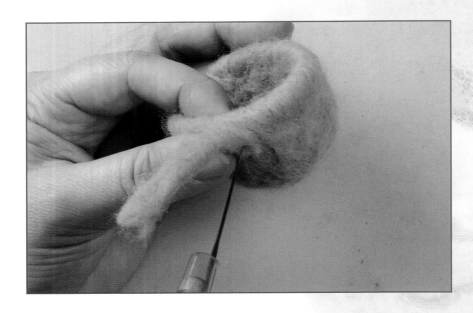

14 Place the end of the handle near the top of the cup, curling it over as shown, and needle it in position.

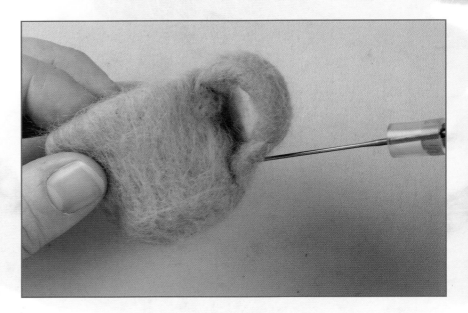

15 Attach the bottom of the handle but do not curl it under this time. Needle to secure it.

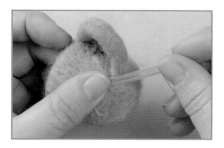

16 Cover any visible joins by adding and needling in more wool.

17 Add a wisp of pale pink wool to create a petal.

18 Make five petals in the same way and add a purple centre to the flower.

19 Add a leaf in dark green and needle it in.

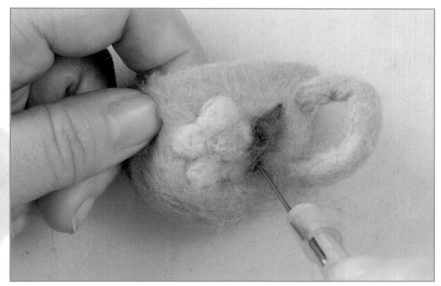

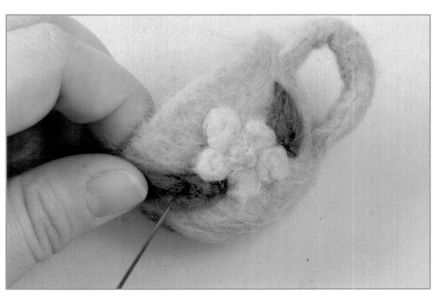

20 Add a second leaf in the same way.

 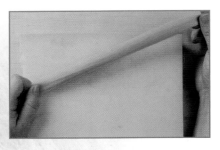 

21 Trim any fluff from the finished cup with scissors.

22 Take a long and fairly thick piece of the same blue wool.

23 Coil it into a spiral shape.

24 Needle the spiral into a flat circle, adding wool to cover the joins, as shown on page 16.

25 Needle the middle of the shape to make the dip in the saucer.

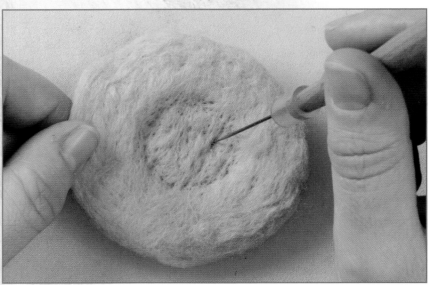

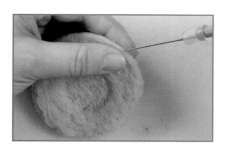

26 Carefully needle the rim of the saucer and refine the circle shape.

27 As with the cup, decorate the saucer with flowers, starting with a pale pink petal.

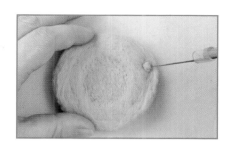

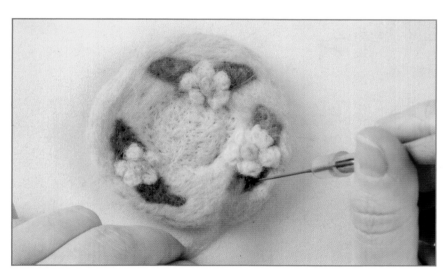

28 Make three flowers, each with five pink petals, a purple centre and two dark green leaves.

The finished cup and saucer.

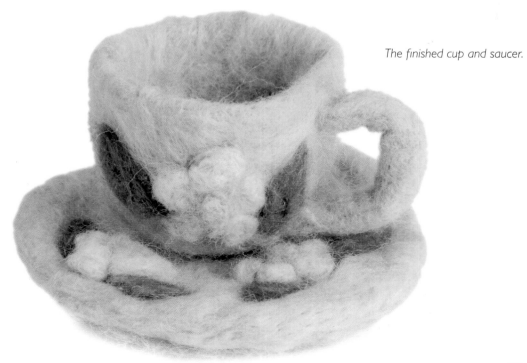

Bowls can be made in the same way as saucers, and a cup can be transformed into a little basket by attaching the handle in a different way. The mug is another alternative, and a ball shape can be decorated to make a delicious looking cake.

These bowls could be used for keeping treasures or jewellery in and could be made in various styles such as Art Deco or Arts and Crafts.

Pink Lady

Figures of this type are often called Waldorf or Steiner style figures as they are commonly made as decorative items to be placed on the Nature or Seasonal table in Steiner kindergartens, where seasons and festivals are celebrated and craft skills and nature are highly revered.

Figures are a lot of fun to make and can be as diverse as your imagination allows, with endless possibilities for hair, clothing and decoration. This figure has curly Wensleydale wool for hair. The figures are quite rustic and naïve in style and unless you feel very confident, avoid felting faces on to the figures as they can be extremely difficult. Faces on Waldorf figures and dolls are generally left blank or very simple so the expression on the face of the figure is left for your imagination to complete.

You will need

- Two pipe cleaners
- Foam block
- Felting needle
- Raw wool
- Merino wool in skin tone, pink, bright green and purple
- Wensleydale wool in mixed colours

1 Twist a pipe cleaner as shown to make the head and arms part of the armature.

2 Fold a second pipe cleaner in half and hook it through the head loop to make the body part of the armature.

3 Twist the second pipe cleaner to secure it in place.

4 Take a piece of raw wool and wind it round a limb of the armature.

5 Wind raw wool around the head and needle it on the foam block.

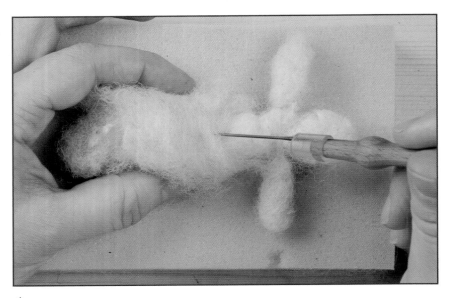

6 Add raw wool to the body and needle it in place.

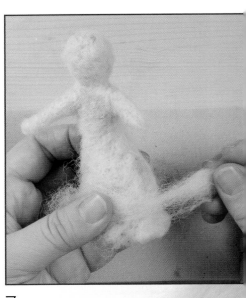

7 Create a wide base to the figure's skirt by adding more raw wool at the bottom.

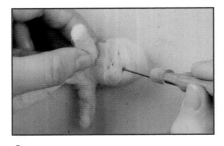

8 Wrap wisps of skin-tone merino wool round the head and needle them in place.

9 Wind thin wisps of the skin-tone merino wool round the arms. Pull them tight and needle them to secure them in place.

10 Wrap pink merino wool round the body to create the dress.

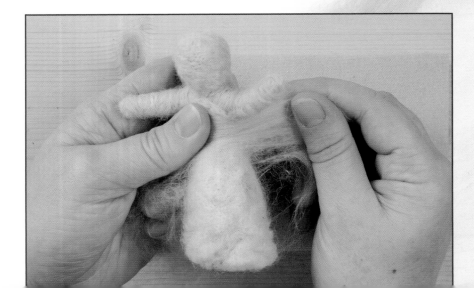

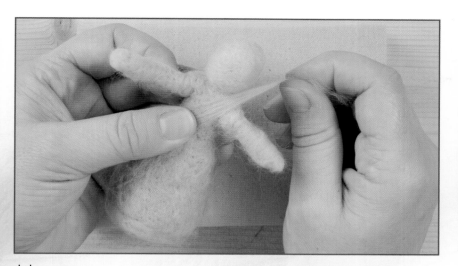

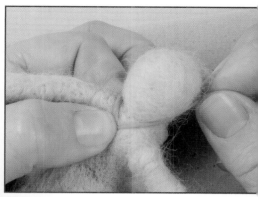

11 Pull wisps of pink merino wool over the shoulders to create the bodice of the dress. Needle it in place.

12 Add a trim round the neckline of the dress with wisps of bright green merino wool, and needle it.

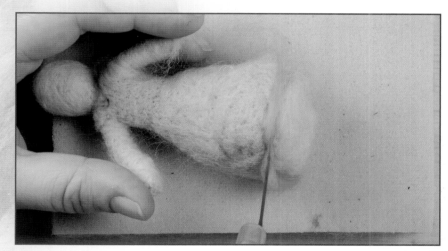

13 Add a trim of the same bright wool round the hem of the dress and needle it in place.

14 Place and needle a waistband for the dress in purple merino wool.

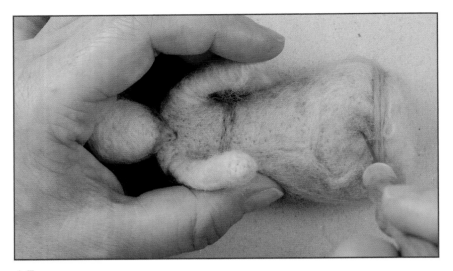

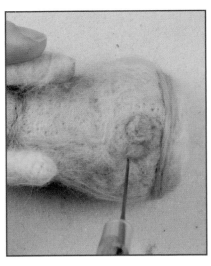

15 Use the same purple merino wool to make a little flower just above the hem of the skirt.

16 Add a leaf in bright green wool at the side of the flower.

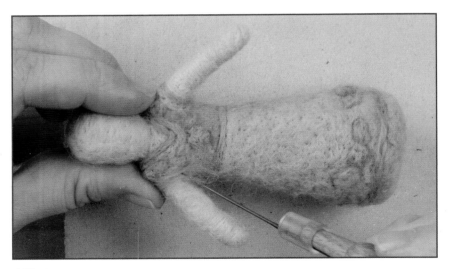

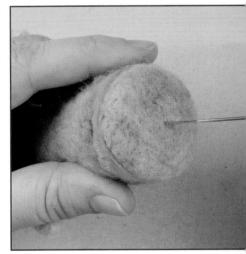

17 Add a second leaf and continue adding flowers all around the hemline. Next add flowers on the bodice of the dress: one in the middle, one on each shoulder, and one on the back of the bodice.

18 Stand the figure up to see if she stands steadily on her base. If not, firm up the base by needling.

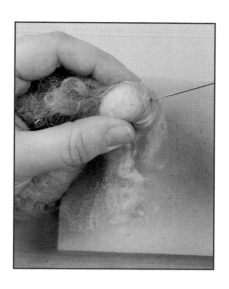

19 Use curly Wensleydale wool for the lady's hair. Pull off wisps of mixed colours, and hold them in the middle. Place the middle against the top of the head, and begin to needle to attach them.

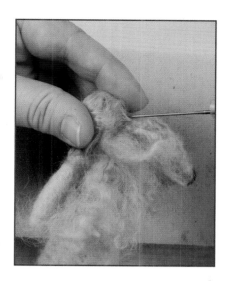

20 Needle the back of the head to attach the hair here too.

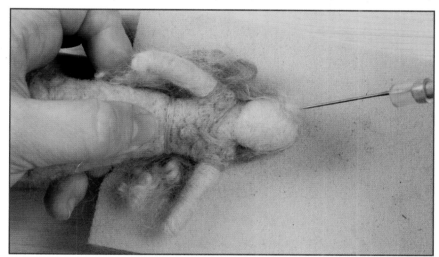

21 Add a flower in the hair to match those on the dress.

22 Add leaves to the flower in the hair.

Figures can be made as large or small as you require and can be in a range of colours to suit different seasons or to become different characters. Why not vary hairstyles or even make up figures that resemble friends and family – no confusion with voodoo intended!

Index